Brave Henry

by M A Clarke

Brave Henry First Edition

Copyright © 2025 Tekamutt Media

All rights reserved.

www.tekamuttmedia.com

ISBN: 978-0-9929585-9-6

Henry is an elephant.

He and his friends all live happily together in the jungle.

Their favourite game is hide and seek.

Every day, they meet in the clearing,
then take turns counting to one hundred,
while everyone else hides.

When he isn't playing,
Henry likes to go for adventures.

He's really good at exploring!

Today, while he is walking through the jungle, he discovers a huge flowing river.

Henry wonders what could be on the other side of the river...

He begins to cross the suspension bridge, taking careful steps one at a time.

When Henry is about half way across the bridge, he notices a missing wooden plank.

He steps over the gap with his long legs and crosses the rest of the bridge.
On the other side, he sees...

... more jungle!

Everything looks the same!

But the sounds are new.

What animals make all these strange noises?

Henry looks up,
and sees...

An adorable little lemur!

The lemur LEAPS from branch to branch. He's very agile!

Something else is in the trees nearby. Henry looks to the right, and sees...

A beautiful bird of paradise!

The bird DIVES from the branch,
and FLAPS her wings.

Henry watches her fly majestically into the sky.

As he continues, Henry suddenly gets the feeling that he is being watched...

He slowly turns around, and sees...

A ferocious tiger!

The tiger POUNCES!

Henry flees as fast as he can!

Henry runs so fast that he flies right over the gap in the bridge!

The tiger isn't paying attention, and he doesn't notice the gap until it's too late!

Henry returns to his friends to tell them all about his adventure. From then on, they call him...

www.ingramcontent.com/pod-product-compliance
Lightning Source LLC
LaVergne TN
LVHW071032070426
835507LV00003B/129